VOGUE® KNITTING
SCARVES

VOGUE KNITTING
SCARVES

SIXTH&SPRING BOOKS
NEW YORK

Sixth&Spring Books
233 Spring Street
New York, New York 10013

Llibrary of Congress Catalonging-in-Publication Data

Vogue knitting scarves/ [edited by Trisha Malcolm]—1st ed.
    p.cm—(Vogue knitting on the go!)
    Reprint. Originally published: New York: Butterick, 1999.
    ISBN 1-931543-21-6
    1. Knitting—Patterns. 2. Scarves. I. Title: Scarves. II. Malcolm, Trisha, 1960-III.
Series.

TT825.V64 2002
746.43'20432--dc21

                                                        2002070780

Manufactured in China

1 3 5 7 9 10 8 6 4 2

TABLE OF CONTENTS

20 POM-POM SCARF
Red hot

22 MOCK CABLE-RIBBED SCARF
Classic complement

24 CABLED CASHMERE SCARF
The luxe touch

26 DIAMOND LEAF SCARF
Understated elegance

30 TEXTURED STRIPE SCARF
Stripe it rich

32 REVERSIBLE APPLIQUÉD WRAP
Turn over a new leaf

34 "FUR" BOA
Go for glamour

36 TRIANGULAR SCARF
Turn-of-the-century elegance

39 CABLED COWL
The "neck" best thing

42 RIBBED BIAS COLLAR
Going around in circles

44 CHEVRON-PATTERNED SCARF
Purple haze

46 GEOMETRIC SCARF
A-maze-ing!

48 SIDEWAYS SCARF
Beyond the fringe

51 LACE AND LEAVES WRAP
Autumn splendor

54 ANTIQUE FAN AND FEATHER STOLE
Waves of blue

56 ROSE LACE STOLE
A modern-day heirloom

60 MOSAIC STOLE
Wrapped in luxury

62 DIAGONAL BLOCK SCARF
It's hip to be square

64 GOSSAMER SHAWL
Diamonds are a girl's best friend

68 RIBBON AND EYELET SCARF
Fringe benefits

70 HOODED SCARF
Take cover

73 LEAF AND CABLE SCARF
Fall foliage

76 FRINGED TURKISH SCARF
Ottoman influence

79 CHILD'S SHEEP SCARF
I love ewe!

82 FAIR ISLE SCARF
Shades of the Shetlands

85 DRAGONFLY SHAWL
The secret garden

INTRODUCTION

Are you too wrapped up in the rush of getting from point A to point B (and everywhere in between) to take time out for the little pleasures in life?... knitting for instance? Well it's time to unwind. Believe it or not, you do have time to knit. You just have to get creative about when and where you pull out your needles.

Scarves are the ultimate on-the-go knitting projects. The investment in time and money is minimal and the simple, structured elegance of most scarf patterns (there's little or no shaping, and certainly no sizing to worry about) makes them perfect for the tiny windows of knitting opportunity that open up during a hectic day. Start on your way to work, fit in a few stitches between appointments (knitting's a great way to make time spent waiting in line fly), and you'll be done in no time.

Scarves are the perfect way to use up odds and ends or splurge on an extra-special something without breaking your budget. Take the yarns listed for each project as suggestions and work your own magic from there, experimenting with new colors and fibers. Just be sure to knit a swatch for gauge before you begin.

So wrap yourself (and your friends and family) in a little handknit luxury. Choose your scarf, grab your needles and get ready to **KNIT ON THE GO!**

THE BASICS

Scarves, and their close relatives the shawl and stole, are probably the oldest forms of outerwear. Born out of necessity, these flat, rectangular pieces of fabric were wrapped around the head, neck, shoulders, or entire body for warmth and modesty. An essential part of clothing throughout history, they have been know by many names: togas to the ancient Romans and Greeks, mantles to the men and women of the Middle Ages. In fact, the word mantle is closely related to the Spanish word mantilla, which means scarf. Through the ages scarves have evolved to become more than just simple items of warm clothing—in some cultures they have been used as symbols of mourning, or have religious or political affiliation. These simple shapes have enjoyed a long history and withstood the test of time, which leads us to today, where they have become one of the hottest fashion items in decades.

Why are scarves so popular with knitters? Because they are one of the easiest items to knit. You just cast on a given number of stitches and knit—no increasing or decreasing. And, you don't have to worry about fitting—just keep knitting until you reach the length you desire. This makes them ideal projects for beginners who are just learning to knit and perfecting their skills. They're also great for "lapsed" knitters who want to brush up on their techniques. Want to test out a yarn you've never worked with before? Or a luxurious fiber you can't afford to buy in quantity? Make a scarf. As knitters increase their knit-knowledge they can try scarves that require shaping, use them to test challenging patterns and intricate color-ways. They're great for experimenting with your own designs, and, they make great gifts!

The varieties of scarves, and the reasons for making them, are nearly endless. With that in mind, we are pleased to present a well-rounded selection to spark your imagination and get you started on making one of these fashion essentials.

SCARF STYLES

Boa

Traditionally made of feathers or fur, this long, narrow scarf is notorious as a dramatic evening accessory. Knitters can recreate its fluffy look using the newest novelty yarns. Go for glamour with our "Fur" Boa on page 34.

Collar

A great accent piece, this short, tubular-shaped scarf gives warmth without clutter. You'll be going round in circles when you try our Ribbed Bias Collar on page 42.

Cowl

Longer and looser than a collar, this tubular-shaped scarf can be draped loosely around the neck or pulled over the head like a hood—it's the "necks" best thing! See our Cabled Cowl on page 39.

GAUGE

Most scarf patterns don't rely on a perfect fit as a knitted garment would, but it is still important to knit a gauge swatch. Without correct gauge a colorwork pattern (such as the Mosaic Stole on page 60) may become distorted. The type of needles used—straight or circular, wood or metal—will influence gauge, so knit your swatch with the needles you plan to use for the project. Measure gauge as illustrated here. Try different needle sizes until your sample measures the required number of stitches and rows. *To get fewer stitches to the inch/cm, use larger needles; to get more stitches to the inch/cm, use smaller needles.*

It's a good idea to keep your gauge swatch in order to test blocking and cleaning methods.

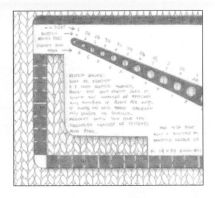

Scarf

Meant to wrap the neck for warmth, this flat, rectangular piece is usually no more than twelve inches (30.5 centimeters) wide, and three to six feet (or meters) in length, but can be any dimension you choose.

Shawl

Rectangular, semi-circular, or triangular in shape, often with a fringed border, the shawl is worn draped around the shoulders. When made in luxurious yarns and patterns, it becomes an elegant evening accessory.

Stole

Wider and longer than a scarf, the stole wraps the torso for warmth. It is a fashionable substitute for a lightweight jacket or sweater. See our Antique Fan and Feather Stole on page 54.

Wrap

The largest member of the scarf family, the wrap is a heavy-weight rectangular piece that is used as outerwear.

FINISHING

Because scarves are frequently knit in one piece, finishing of the garment must be considered from the onset. We've included some helpful hints to remember when beginning your scarf project.

1. Because the back-side of the fabric will be seen when the scarf is wrapped around your body, you must be ready for the reverse side to be on display. Think about using a stitch that is reversible, or one which looks good on both sides.

2. Consider adding border stitches to your scarf so that the garment has a built-in finish (many border stitches will also help the fabric lie flat).

3. When adding a new yarn, be careful to do so in a place where you can easily weave the end into the garment, as there is frequently no "wrong side" on a scarf.

4. Knitting a scarf twice as wide as necessary is one way to ensure extra warmth as well as a clean finish. Just fold over and sew up along the seam for a cozy and completely reversible wrap.

5. Consider adding a luxurious fabric lining as an elegant accent to your fine handwork, as we did in the Mosaic Stole on page 60.

YARN SELECTION

For an exact reproduction of the scarf photographed, use the yarn listed in the materials section of the pattern. We've selected yarns that are readily available in the U.S. and Canada at the time of printing. The Resources list on page 94 provides addresses of yarn distributors. Contact them for the name of a retailer in your area.

YARN SUBSTITUTION

You may wish to substitute yarns. Perhaps a spectacular yarn matches your new coat, maybe you view small-scale projects as a chance to incorporate leftovers from your yarn stash, or the yarn specified may not be available in your area. Scarves allow you to be as creative as you like, but you'll need to knit to the given gauge to obtain the knitted measurements with the substitute yarn (see "Gauge" on page 11). Make pattern adjustments where necessary. Be sure to consider how different yarn types (chenille, mohair, bouclé, etc.) will affect the final appearance of your scarf, and how they will feel against your skin. Also take fiber care into consideration, some yarns can be machine or hand

---

YARN SYMBOLS

① **Fine Weight**
(29-32 stitches per 4"/10cm)
Includes baby and fingering yarns, and some of the heavier crochet cottons. The range of needle sizes is 0-4 (2-3.5mm).

② **Lightweight**
(25-28 stitches per 4"/10cm)
Includes sport yarn, sock yarn, UK 4-ply and lightweight DK yarns. The range of needle sizes is 3-6 (3-4mm).

③ **Medium Weight**
(21-24 stitches per 4"/10cm)
Includes DK and worsted, the most commonly used knitting yarns. The range of needle sizes is 6-9 (4-5.5mm).

④ **Medium-heavy Weight**
(17-20 stitches per 4"/10cm)
Also called heavy worsted or Aran. The range of needle sizes is 8-10 (5-6mm).

⑤ **Bulky Weight**
(13-16 stitches per 4"/10cm)
Also called chunky. Includes heavier Icelandic yarns. The range of needle sizes is 10-11 (6-8mm).

⑥ **Extra-bulky Weight**
(9-12 stitches per 4"/10cm)
The heaviest yarns available. The range of needle sizes is 11 and up (8mm and up).

washed, others will require dry cleaning.

To facilitate yarn substitution, *Vogue Knitting* grades yarn by the standard stitch gauge obtained in Stockinette stitch. You'll find a grading number in the "Materials" section of the pattern, immediately following the fiber type of the yarn. Look for a substitute yarn that falls into the same category. The suggested needle size and gauge on the ball band should be comparable to that on the Yarn Symbols chart on page 12.

After you've successfully gauge-swatched a substitute yarn, you'll need to figure out how much of the substitute yarn the project requires. First, find the total length of the original yarn in the pattern (multiply number of balls by yards/meters per ball). Divide this figure by the new yards/meters per ball (listed on the ball band). Round up to the next whole number. The answer is the number of balls required.

FOLLOWING CHARTS

Charts provide a convenient way to follow colorwork, lace, cable and other stitch patterns at a glance. *Vogue Knitting* stitch charts utilize the universal knitting language of "symbolcraft." Unless otherwise indicated, read charts from right to left on right side (RS) rows and from left to right on wrong side (WS) rows, repeating any stitch and row repeats as directed in the pattern. Posting a self-adhesive note under your working row is an easy way to keep track of your place on a chart.

COLORWORK KNITTING

Two main types of colorwork are explored in this book.

Intarsia

Intarsia is accomplished with separate bobbins of individual colors. This method is ideal for large blocks of color or for motifs that aren't repeated close together. When changing colors, always pick up the new color and wrap around the old color to prevent holes.

Stranding

When motifs are closely placed, colorwork is accomplished by stranding along two or more colors per row, creating "floats" on the wrong side of the fabric. When using this method, twist yarns on WS to prevent holes and strand loosely to keep knitting from puckering.

Note that yarn amounts have been calculated for the colorwork method suggested in the pattern. Knitting a stranded pattern with intarsia bobbins will take less yarn, while stranding an intarsia pattern will require more yarn.

BLOCKING

Blocking is the best way to shape pattern pieces and smooth knitted edges. However, some yarns, such as chenilles and ribbons, do not benefit from blocking. Choose a blocking method according to the yarn care label and, when in doubt, test-block on your gauge swatch.

Wet Block Method

Using rust-proof pins, pin scarf to measurements on a flat surface and lightly dampen using a spray bottle. Allow to dry before removing pins.

Steam Block Method

Pin scarf to measurements with wrong side of knitting facing up. Steam lightly, holding the iron 2"/5cm above the work. Do not press the iron onto the knitting, as it will flatten the stitches.

CARE

Refer to the yarn label for the recommended cleaning method. Many of the scarves in the book can be washed by hand (or in the machine on a gentle or wool cycle) in lukewarm water with a mild detergent. Do not agitate, and don't soak for more than 10 minutes. Rinse gently with tepid water, then fold in a towel and gently press the water out. Lay flat to dry, away from excessive heat and light.

WORKING WITH RIBBON YARNS

■ Place a nylon spool protector (a tube of netting) or a tube cut from an old stocking around your ball of ribbon so it won't unwind too fast. Slinky ribbon yarns side off the ball very easily causing tangles or knots.

■ Avoid pulling the ribbon. Keep a light hold as ribbons have a great deal of stretch and can distort when pulled.

■ As with chenille, avoid over-twisting. A ribbon will have the best appearance when it lays flat.

■ Clean your hands before knitting. Natural oils may stain or stiffen the rayon fiber used in most ribbons and some chenilles.

■ Use non-slip needles. Needles of bamboo or wood will give you more control when working with slippery yarns.

FRINGE

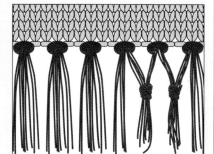

SIMPLE FRINGE: Cut yarn twice desired length plus extra for knotting. On wrong side, insert hook from front to back through piece and over folded yarn. Pull yarn through. Draw ends through and tighten. Trim yarn.

KNOTTED FRINGE: After working a simple fringe (it should be longer to allow for extra knotting), take one half of the strands from each fringe and knot them with half the strands from the neighboring fringe.

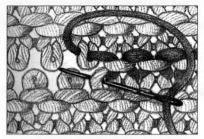

I Insert yarn needle purlwise into the first stitch on the front piece, then purlwise into the first stitch on the back piece. Draw the yarn through.

2 Insert yarn needle knitwise into the first stitch on the front piece again. Draw the yarn through.

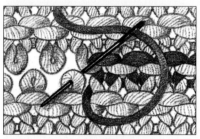

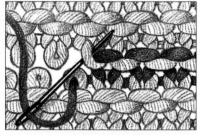

3 Insert yarn needle purlwise into the next stitch on the front piece. Draw the yarn through.

4 Insert yarn needle knitwise into the first stitch on the back piece again. Draw the yarn through.

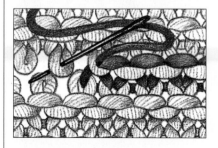

5 Insert yarn needle purlwise into the next stitch on the back piece. Draw the yarn through. Repeat steps 2 through 5.

WORKING A YARN OVER

There are different ways to make a yarn over. Which method to use depends on where you are in the stitch pattern. If you do not make the yarn over in the right way, you may lose it on the following row, or make a yarn over that is too big. Here are the different variations:

Between two knit stitches: Bring the yarn from the back of the work to the front between the two needles. Knit the next stitch, bringing the yarn to the back over the right-hand needle, as shown.

Between a knit and a purl stitch: Bring the yarn from the back to the front between the two needles. Then bring it to the back over the right-hand needle and back to the front again, as shown. Purl the next stitch.

Between a purl and a knit stitch: Leave the yarn at the front of the work. Knit the next stitch, bringing the yarn to the back over the right-hand needle, as shown.

Between two purl stitches: Leave the yarn at the front of the work. Bring the yarn to the back over the right-hand needle and to the front again, as shown. Purl the next stitch.

Multiple yarn overs (two or more): Wrap the yarn around the needle, as when working a single yarn over, then continue wrapping the yarn around the needle as many times as indicated. Work the next stitch of the left-hand needle. On the following row, work stitches into the extra yarn overs as described in the pattern. The illustration at right depicts a finished yarn-over on the purl side.

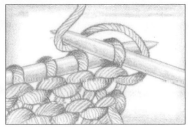

At the beginning of a knit row: Insert the right-hand needle knitwise into the first stitch on the left-hand needle, keeping the yarn in front of the needle. Bring the yarn over the right-hand needle to the back and knit the first stitch, holding the yarn over with your thumb if necessary.

At the beginning of a purl row: Insert the right-hand needle purlwise into the first stitch on the left-hand needle, keeping the yarn behind the needle. Purl the first stitch.

STEM STITCH

Bring needle up on edge of area to be outlined. Insert it a short distance to the right at an angle and pull it through, emerging at the midpoint of the previous stitch. Work left to right, keeping the thread below the needle.

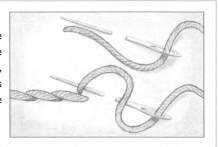

DUPLICATE STITCH

Duplicate stitch covers a knit stitch. Bring the needle up below the stitch to be worked. Insert the needle under both loops one row above and pull it through. Insert it back into the stitch below and through the center of the next stitch in one motion, as shown.

KNITTING TERMS AND ABBREVIATIONS

approx approximately

beg begin(ning)

bind off Used to finish an edge and keep stitches from unraveling. Lift the first stitch over the second, the second over the third, etc. (UK: cast off)

cast on A foundation row of stitches placed on the needle in order to begin knitting.

CC contrast color

ch chain(s)

cm centimeter(s)

cn cable needle

cont continu(e)(ing)

dec decrease(ing)—Reduce the stitches in a row (knit 2 together).

dpn double pointed needle(s)

foll follow(s)(ing)

g gram(s)

garter stitch Knit every row. Circular knitting: knit one round, then purl one round.

inc increase(ing)—Add stitches in a row (knit into the front and back of a stitch).

k knit

k2tog knit 2 stitches together

LH left-hand

lp(s) loops(s)

m meter(s)

M1 make one stitch—With the needle tip, lift the strand between last stitch worked and next stitch on the left-hand needle and knit into the back of it. One stitch has been added.

M1 p-st With the needle tip, lift the strand between last stitch worked and next stitch on the left hand needle and purl it. One purl stitch has been added.

MC main color

mm millimeter(s)

no stitch On some charts, "no stitch" is indicated with shaded spaces where stitches have been decreased or not yet made. In such cases, work the stitches of the chart, skipping over the "no stitch" spaces.

oz ounce(s)

p purl

p2tog purl 2 stitches together

pat(s) pattern

pick up and knit (purl) Knit (or purl) into the loops along an edge.

pm place marker(s)—Place or attach a loop of contrast yarn or purchased stitch marker as indicated.

psso pass slip stitch(es) over

rem remain(s)(ing)

rep repeat

rev St st reverse Stockinette stitch-Purl right-side rows, knit wrong-side rows. Circular knitting: purl all rounds. (UK: reverse stocking stitch)

rnd(s) round(s)

RH right-hand

RS right side(s)

sc single crochet (UK: dc—double crochet)

sk skip

SKP Slip 1, knit 1, pass slip stitch over knit 1. One stitch has been decreased.

SK2P Slip 1, knit 2 together, pass slip stitch over the knit 2 together. Two stitches have been decreased.

sl slip-An unworked stitch made by passing a stitch from the left-hand to the right-hand needle as if to purl.

sl st slip stitch (UK: sc—single crochet)

ssk slip, slip, knit—Slip next 2 stitches knitwise, one at a time, to right-hand needle. Insert tip of left-hand needle into fronts of these stitches from left to right. Knit them together. One stitch has been decreased.

sssk Slip next 3 sts knitwise, one at a time, to right hand needle. Insert tip of left-hand needle into fronts of these stitches from left to right. Knit them together. Two stitches have been decreased.

st(s) stitch(es)

St st Stockinette stitch—Knit right-side rows, purl wrong-side rows. Circular knitting: knit all rounds. (UK: stocking stitch)

tbl through back of loop

tog together

WS wrong side(s)

wyib with yarn in back

wyif with yarn in front

work even Continue in pattern without increasing or decreasing. (UK: work straight)

yd yard(s)

yo yarn over-Make a new stitch by wrapping the yarn over the right-hand needle. (UK: yfwd, yon, yrn)

* = repeat directions following * as many times as indicated.

[ ] = Repeat directions inside brackets as many times as indicated.

POM-POMS

POM-POM TEMPLATE

1 Following the template, cut two circular pieces of cardboard.

2 Hold the two circles together and wrap the yarn tightly around the cardboard several times. Secure and carefully cut the yarn.

3 Tie a piece a yarn tightly between the two circles. Remove the cardboard and trim the pom-pom to the desired size.

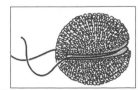

POM-POM SCARF
Red hot

Cozy basket-rib stitches insulate against the cold weather, while cheeky pom-poms cheerfully chase away the winter blues. Designed by Barbara Fimbel.

KNITTED MEASUREMENTS
■ Approx 10" x 60"/25.5cm x 152cm

MATERIALS
■ 7 1¾oz/50g hanks (each approx 116yd/105m) of Classic Elite *Inca Alpaca* (alpaca④) in #1158 red
■ 1 extra hank for making pom-poms
■ One pair size 6 (4mm) needles *or size to obtain gauge*

GAUGE
27 sts and 36 rows to 4"/10cm over pat st using size 6 (4mm) needles.
Take time to check gauge.

PATTERN STITCH
(over an odd number of sts)
Row 1 (RS) Knit.
Row 2 Purl.
Row 3 K1, *sl 1 purlwise, k1; rep from * to end.
Row 4 K1, *wyif, sl 1 purlwise, yarn to back, k1; rep from * to end.
Rep rows 1-4 for pat st.

SCARF
Cast on 65 sts. Work in garter st for 1"/2.5cm.
Beg pat st
Next row (RS) K2, work pat st to last 2 sts, k2. Cont in pat as established, keeping first and last 2 sts in garter st, until piece measures 59"/149.5cm from beg, end with row 1 of pat. Work in garter st for 1"/2.5cm more. Bind off.

FINISHING
Block scarf. Make eight 2"/5cm pom-poms. Sew 4 evenly spaced at each end of scarf.

MOCK CABLE-RIB SCARF

Classic complement

Very Easy Very Vogue

A timeless accessory knit in a soft "felted" wool. Susan Mills' sporty mock cable-rib scarf will appeal to the most discerning of tastes.

KNITTED MEASUREMENTS

- Approx 9½" x 49"/24cm x 124.5cm

MATERIALS

- 3 1¾oz/50g balls (each approx 120yd/108m) of Adrienne Vittadini/JCA *Aria* (wool/nylon⑤) in #921 rust
- One pair size 8 (5mm) needles *or size to obtain gauge*

GAUGE

19 sts and 22 rows to 4"/10cm over pat st using size 8 (5mm) needles.
Take time to check gauge.

PATTERN STITCH

(multiple of 4 sts plus 2)

Row 1 (RS) *P2, k2; rep from *, end p2.

Rows 2 and 4 *K2, p2, rep from *, end k2.

Row 3 *P2, k2tog without slipping sts from needle, then k first st again, drop both sts from needle; rep from *, end p2.

Rep rows 1-4 for pat st.

SCARF

Cast on 46 sts. Work in pat st for 49"/124.5cm or desired length. Bind off.

FINISHING

Block scarf.

CABLED CASHMERE SCARF

The luxe touch

The ultimate winter warmer. Lush cashmere looks and feels divine in a pattern of alternating cable and ladder stitches. Designed by Barry Klein.

KNITTED MEASUREMENTS

▪ Approx 8" x 58"/20.5cm x 147cm (without fringe)

MATERIALS

▪ 2 3½oz/100g hanks (each approx 165yd/152m) of Trendsetter Yarns *Dali* (cashmere⑤) in #3 creme
▪ One pair size 10 (6mm) needles *or size to obtain gauge*
▪ Size G/6 (4.5mm) crochet hook
▪ Cable needle

GAUGES

▪ 7 sts to 1¾"/4.5cm and 20 rows to 4"/10cm over ladder st using size 10 (6mm) needles.
▪ 10 sts to 1½"/4cm over large cable using size 10 (6mm) needles.
Take time to check gauges.

Note Before beg, wind off 25yd/23m on one hank for crochet and fringe.

STITCH GLOSSARY
Ladder Stitch
Row 1 (RS) Knit.
Row 2 *P1, k1; rep from *, end p1.

Rep rows 1 and 2 for ladder st.
Small Cable
(over 6 sts)
Rows 1, 5, 7 and 9 (RS) P1, k4, p1.
Row 2 and all WS rows K1, p4, k1.
Row 3 P1, sl 2 sts to cn and hold to *back*, k2, k2 from cn, p1.
Row 10 Rep row 2.
Rep rows 1-10 for small cable.
Large Cable
(over 10 sts)
Rows 1, 5, 7 and 9 (RS) P2, k6, p2.
Row 2 and all WS rows K2, p6, k2.
Row 3 P2, sl 3 sts to cn and hold to *back*, k3, k3 from cn, p2.
Row 10 Rep row 2.
Rep rows 1-10 for large cable.

SCARF
Cast on 40 sts. Work as foll: 2 sts in garter st, 6 sts in small cable, 7 sts in ladder st, 10 sts in large cable, 7 sts in ladder st, 6 sts in small cable, 2 sts in garter st. Cont in pats as established until you run out of yarn. Piece measures approx 58"/147cm. Bind off in pat.

FINISHING
Block scarf.
Fringe
With RS facing and crochet hook, work 1 row of sc along cast-on and bound-off edges. Make fringe with rem yarn and knot in place.

For Expert Knitters

Short rows and textural lace stitches form exquisite diamonds to trim the ends of Margaret Stove's chic, garter-stitch scarf. Cashmere and silk add a touch of luxury to this timeless treasure

KNITTED MEASUREMENTS
■ Approx 8½" x 62"/21.5cm x 157cm (measured from the longest point)

MATERIALS
■ 6 .88oz/25g balls (each approx 92yd/85m) of Baruffa/Lane Borgosesia *Cash Silk* (wool/silk/cashmere②) in #25601 lavender
■ One pair size 5 (3.75mm) needles *or size to obtain gauge*
■ Stitch holder

GAUGE
28 sts and 40 rows to 4"/10cm over garter st using size 5 (3.75mm) needles.
Take time to check gauge.

Notes 1) Scarf is made in two pieces and grafted tog at the center. **2)** When slipping sts, always hold yarn to back.

STITCH GLOSSARY
P2SSO
Pass 2 slipped sts over k st.

SCARF
Cast on 49 sts very loosely. K 3 rows.
Beg diamond leaf chart
Row 1 (RS) K21, work row 1 of chart as foll: k2tog, yo, sl 2, k1, p2sso, yo, k2tog. Turn.
Row 2 Sl 1, k3, k2tog. Turn.
Cont in this way to work short rows foll chart through row 42—59 sts. Cont to work even in chart pat through row 83. Cont in garter st on all sts for 22"/56cm more. Place sts on a holder.
Work a 2nd piece in same way.

FINISHING
Block pieces. Weave sts on holder tog (see "Grafting on Garter Stitch" on page 17).

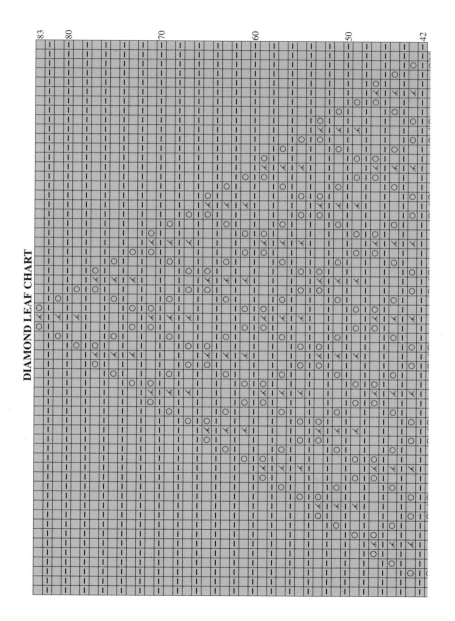

DIAMOND LEAF CHART

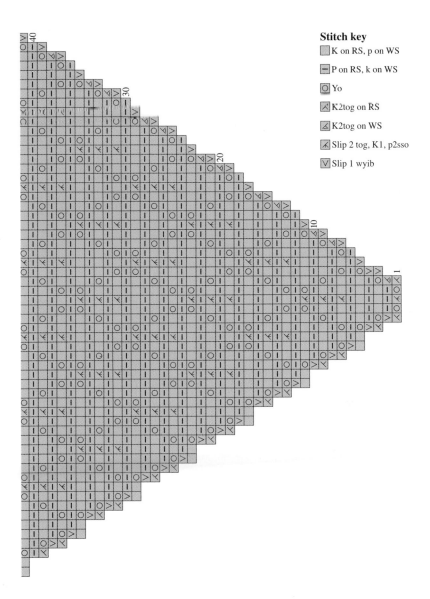

Stitch key

- K on RS, p on WS
- P on RS, k on WS
- Yo
- K2tog on RS
- K2tog on WS
- Slip 2 tog, K1, p2sso
- Slip 1 wyib

Irina Poludnenko creates tone-on-tone textural contrast by alternating garter-stitch bands of rayon tape and rayon chenille.

KNITTED MEASUREMENTS
- Approx 8" x 66"/20.5cm x 167.5cm (without fringe)

MATERIALS
- 2 1¾oz/50g skeins (each approx 77yd/71m) of Berroco, Inc. *Chinchilla* (rayon④) in #5534 berry (A)
- 3 1¾oz/50g skeins (each approx 75yd/69m) of *Glacé* (rayon④) in #2534 berry (B)
- One pair size 5 (3.75mm) needles *or size to obtain gauge*

GAUGES
- 18 sts and 23 rows to 4"/10cm over garter st using size 5 (3.75mm) needles and A.
- 18 sts and 25 rows to 4"/10cm over garter st using size 5 (3.75mm) needles and B.

Take time to check gauges.

SCARF
With A, cast on 35 sts and work in garter st as foll: *20 rows A, 22 rows B; rep from * (42 rows) 8 times more. K 20 rows A. Bind off.

FINISHING
Block piece.

Fringe
Cut 15"/38cm strands of B. Using 2 strands for each fringe, attach fringe to each end of scarf. Trim ends.

Knitted leaf appliqués trim both sides of Nicky Epstein's whimsical basketweave scarf. Dimensional leaves dangle from I-cords, creating a fanciful fringe.

KNITTED MEASUREMENTS
■ Approx 13" x 60"/33cm x 152cm (without fringe)

MATERIALS
■ 4 1¾oz/50g balls (each approx 165yd/150m) of Garnstudio/Aurora Yarns *Karisma Angora-Tweed* (angora/lambswool④) in #03 blue (MC)
■ 3 balls in #04 green (CC)
■ One pair size 7 (4.5mm) needles *or size to obtain gauge*
■ Two size 7 (4.5mm) dpn

GAUGE
20 sts and 26 rows to 4"/10cm over St st using size 7 (4.5mm) needles.
Take time to check gauge.

Note Leaves are made separately and sewn on after scarf is knit.

BASKETWEAVE PATTERN
(over 60 sts)
Row 1 (RS) [K15, p15] twice.
Row 2 K the knit sts and p the purl sts.
Rows 3-18 Rep rows 1 and 2 eight times.
Row 19 [P15, k15] twice.
Row 20 Rep row 2.
Rows 21-36 Rep rows 19 and 20 eight times.
Rep rows 1-36 for basketweave pat.

SCARF
With MC, cast on 68 sts. K 2 rows.

Beg basketweave pat
Row 1 (RS) Work 4 sts in k1, p1 rib, work

basketweave pat over next 60 sts, work 4 sts in k1, p1 rib. Cont pat as established until 36 rows of basketweave pat have been worked 10 times, then work rows 1-18 once more. K 2 rows. Bind off all sts.

APPLIED LEAVES
(make 84)
With CC and dpn, cast on 3 sts.

I-Cord
K3 *do NOT turn work. Slide sts to beg of needle and pulling yarn to tighten, k3; rep from * for I-cord for ¾"/2cm, inc 1 st each end of last row—5 sts. Change to straight needles.

Leaf
Row 1 (RS) K2, yo, k1, yo, k2—7 sts.
Row 2 and all WS rows Purl.
Row 3 K3, yo, k1, yo, k3—9 sts.
Row 5 K4, yo, k1, yo, k4—11 sts.
Row 7 Ssk, k7, k2tog—9 sts.
Row 9 Ssk, k5, k2tog—7 sts.
Row 11 Ssk, k3, k2tog—5 sts.
Row 13 Ssk, k1, k2tog—3 sts.
Row 15 SK2P.
Fasten off.

FINISHING
Block piece. Sew leaves onto rev St st squares on front and back of scarf, vary direction of leaves if desired.

Leaf fringe
(make 18)
With MC and dpn, cast on 3 sts. Work I-cord as for applied leaves for 1½"/4cm, inc 1 st each end of last row—5 sts. Change to straight needles and CC and work leaf.
With CC, cast on 5 sts and make a 2nd leaf. Sew to first leaf with WS tog.
Attach 9 fringe to each end of scarf.

"FUR" BOA

Go for glamour

Simple garter stitch takes a whimsical turn in fluffy hand-dyed rayon "fur." A quick-and-easy knit, designed by Gotta Knit!, a New York City yarn store.

KNITTED MEASUREMENTS
- Approx 5½" x 44"/14cm x 111.5cm

MATERIALS
- 1 1¾oz/50g ball (each approx 82yd/74m) of Great Adirondack Co. *Fluff* (rayon③) in tiffany
- One pair size 17 (12.75mm) needles *or size to obtain gauge*

GAUGE
14 sts to 4"/10cm over garter st using size 17 (12.75mm) needles.
Take time to check gauge.

Note Only st gauge is given. Length of scarf may vary depending on your individual row gauge.

SCARF
Cast on 20 sts. Work in garter st until approx 1yd/1m is left. Bind off all sts. Weave in ends. Do not block.

Simple shaping creates a quick-and-easy classic with ends long enough to drape, knot or pin in front. The lace edging is knit at the same time as the body; designed by Evelyn Clark.

KNITTED MEASUREMENTS

■ Approx 12½"/31.5cm at center back, sides are 28"/71cm long

MATERIALS

■ 1 2oz/54g ball (each approx 180yd/166m) of Fingerlakes Woolen Mill *Angora Luxury 2 Ply* (wool/angora④) in teal

■ One pair size 7 (4.5mm) needles *or size to obtain gauge*

■ Stitch markers and holders

GAUGE

14 sts and 28 rows to 4"/10cm over garter st using size 7 (4.5mm) needles.

Take time to check gauge.

Note It is helpful to use different colored markers to distinguish between odd and even numbered rows.

SCARF

Bottom point

Cast on 2 sts.

Row 1 Knit.

Row 2 Inc 1 (k into front and back of st), k1—3 sts.

Rows 3 and 4 Knit.

Row 5 K1, inc 1, k1—4 sts.

Rows 6 and 7 Knit.

Body

Row 1 Inc 1, k1, yo, k1, inc 1—7 sts.

Row 2 and all even rows Knit.

Row 3 Inc 1, k2, pm, yo, k1, yo, pm, k2, inc 1—11 sts.

Row 5 Ssk, k2, sl marker, yo, k3, yo, sl marker, k2, k2tog—11 sts.

Row 7 Ssk, k1, sl marker, yo, k5, yo, sl marker, k1, k2tog—11 sts.

Row 9 Inc 1, k1, sl marker, yo, k to marker, yo, sl marker, k1, inc 1—15 sts.

Row 11 Inc 1, k2, sl marker, yo, k to marker, yo, sl marker, k2, inc 1—19 sts.

Row 13 Ssk, k2, sl marker, yo, k to marker, yo, sl marker, k2, k2tog—19 sts.

Row 15 Ssk, k1, sl marker, yo, k to marker, yo, sl marker, k1, k2tog—19 sts.

Row 16 Knit.

Rep rows 9-16 until there are 79 sts between markers, end with row 16—83 sts.

Neck shaping

Inc 1, k1, sl marker, yo, k25, bind off 29 sts, k to marker, yo, sl marker, k1, inc 1—29 sts each side.

Put 29 right tie sts onto holder.

Left tie

K 1 row.

Beg tie shaping

Row 1 K1, k3tog tbl, k to marker, yo, sl marker, k2, inc 1—29 sts.

Row 2 and all even rows Knit.

Row 3 K1, k3tog tbl, k to marker, yo, sl marker, k2, k2tog—27 sts.

Row 5 K1, k3tog tbl, k to marker, yo, sl marker, k1, k2tog—25 sts.

Row 7 K1, k3tog tbl, k to marker, yo, sl marker, k1, inc 1—25 sts.

Row 8 Knit.

Rep rows 1-8 until 5 sts rem, end with row 6.

Tie end

Row 1 K3tog tbl, yo, remove marker, k2tog—3 sts.

Row 2 Knit.

Row 3 K3tog. Fasten off.

Right tie

Put 29 right tie sts onto needles. K 1 row.

Beg tie shaping

Row 1 Inc 1, k2, sl marker, yo, k to last 4 sts, k3tog, k1—29 sts.

Row 2 and all even rows Knit.

Row 3 Ssk, k2, sl marker, yo, k to last 4 sts, k3tog, k1—27 sts.

Row 5 Ssk, k1, sl marker, yo, k to last 4 sts, k3tog, k1—25 sts.

Row 7 Inc 1, k1, sl marker, yo, k to last 4 sts, k3tog, k1—25 sts.

Row 8 Knit.

Rep rows 1-8 until 5 sts rem, end with row 6.

Tie end

Row 1 Ssk, remove marker, yo, k3tog—3 sts.

Row 2 Knit.

Row 3 K3tog tbl. Fasten off.

FINISHING

Block, pinning out points on lace edging.

CABLED COWL
The "neck" best thing

Cuddle up with Wendy Sacks' practical sideways cowl in a broken-rib and center-cable pattern. Hand-dyed New Zealand wool ensures warmth and style.

KNITTED MEASUREMENTS

■ Approx 12"/30.5 wide x 14"/35.5cm high

MATERIALS

■ 1 8oz/250g hank (each approx 310yd/286m) of Wool Pak NZ/Baabajoes Wool Co. *Woolpak 14 Ply* (wool⑥) in fall foliage

■ One pair size 10½ (6.5mm) needles *or size to obtain gauge*

■ Size K/10½ (7mm) crochet hook

■ Cable needle

■ Stitch markers

GAUGE

18 sts and 20 rows to 4"/10cm over broken rib using size 10½ (6.5mm) needles. *Take time to check gauge.*

Note Cowl is knit sideways and seamed in back with slits at shoulders.

STITCH GLOSSARY

12-Stitch Left Cable (12-st LC)

Sl 6 sts to cn and hold to *front*, k6, k6 from cn.

SCARF

Cast on 60 sts.

Beg chart pats

Row 1 (RS) Work 24 sts right-slanting broken rib chart, pm, 12 sts cable chart, pm, 24 sts left-slanting broken rib chart. Cont in pats as established, slipping markers every row, until piece measures 5½"/14cm from beg.

Shoulder slit

Next row (RS) Bind off 18 sts, work to end.

Next row Work 42 sts, cast on 18 sts. Work even until piece measures 16½"/42cm from beg, end with a WS row. Work 2nd shoulder slit as for first. Work even until piece measures 24"/61cm from beg. Bind off.

FINISHING

Block scarf. Sew cast-on and bound-off edges tog for back seam. With RS facing and crochet hook, work 1 row sl st along shoulder slits.

LEFT-SLANTING BROKEN RIB

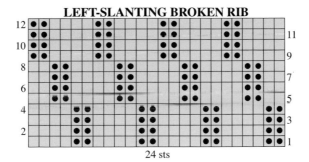

24 sts

CABLE CHART

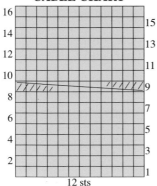

12 sts

Stitch key

☐ K on RS, p on WS

◉ P on RS, k on WS

▨ 12-st LC

RIGHT-SLANTING BROKEN RIB

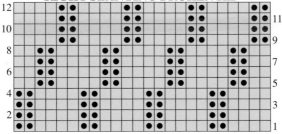

24 sts

RIBBED BIAS COLLAR

Going around in circles

For Experienced Knitters

A fun-to-knit tube collar worked in a doubled alpaca-blend yarn finishes quickly on extra-large needles. Short rows and ingenious bias shaping give this scarf a very versatile wearability. Designed by Mari Lynn Patrick.

KNITTED MEASUREMENTS
▧ Approx 18"/45.5cm at neck, 36"/91cm at lower edge and 11"/28cm deep

MATERIALS
▧ 4 1¾oz/50g balls (each approx 107yd/98m) of Lion Brand AL•PA•KA (acrylic/wool/alpaca④) in #149 silver grey
▧ One pair size 11 (8mm) needles *or size to obtain gauge*
▧ Size K/10½ (7mm) crochet hook

GAUGE
14 sts and 16 rows to 4"/10cm over k2, p3 rib using double strand of yarn and size 11 (8mm) needles.
Take time to check gauge.

COLLAR
Beg at bias short end, with double strand of yarn and size 11 (8mm) needles, cast on 4 sts.
Row 1 (RS) K3, p1.
Row 2 (WS) K into back and front of first st, (inc), p2, k1 (selvage st).
Row 3 K3, p1, p into back and front of last st (inc).
Row 4 P1 and k1 into first st, k2, p2, k1.
Row 5 K3, p3, k into back and front of last st—8 sts. Cont in this way to add sts in k2, p3 rib at end of every RS row and beg of every WS row (with k1 selvage at opposite end) until there are a total of 37 sts. Place a yarn marker (1) at end of last RS row. Cont with a k1 selvage st at each end of row, work even in rib for 5 more rows.

Beg short-row shaping
*Short row 1 (WS) Work to last 8 sts, turn.
Next row (RS) Sl 1, work to end. To close up hole: With LH needle, pick up side of k st 2 rows below st on RH needle, p2tog tbl to close hole. Work 4 rows even on all sts.
Short row 2 (WS) Work to last 18 sts, turn.
Next row Sl 1, work to end. Work 4 rows even.
Short row 3 (WS) Work 9 sts (leave rem 28 sts unworked), turn.
Next row Sl 1, rib to end. Work 4 rows even*. Rep between *'s twice more. Rep short row 1 and next row. Place yarn marker (2) at end of last RS row. Work even for 24 rows or 6"/15cm from yarn marker (2), place a yarn marker (3) at end of last RS row.
**Next row (WS) Bind off 4 sts, work to end.
Next row Work to last st, sl last st. Rep from ** 7 times more. Bind off rem 5 sts.

FINISHING
Block lightly to measurements. Place a yarn marker (4) at 12"/30cm from cast-on sts along side edge of bias front edge (see schematic). Sew shaped bound-off edge to the 12"/30cm marked edge. With crochet hook and double strand of yarn (from marker 1 to marker 3), work an edge of sc along back edge only, working from RS into 3rd st from end of each row.

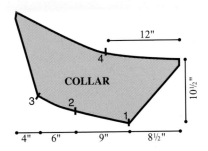

Designer Lipp Holmfeld puts a clever new twist on the basic chevron pattern. Two plum-perfect shades, a solid and a space-dyed, create the striking stripes.

KNITTED MEASUREMENTS

■ Approx 80" x 24"/203cm x 61cm (without fringe)

MATERIALS

■ 6 1¾oz/50g balls (each approx 173yd/160m) of Cleckheaton/Plymouth *Flowerdale 8 Ply* (mohair/wool/nylon④) each in #4 purple (A) and #15 blue multi (B)

■ One pair size 7 (4.5mm) needles *or size to obtain gauge*

■ Stitch holder

GAUGE

18 sts and 36 rows to 4"/10cm over garter st using size 7 (4.5mm) needles.

Take time to check gauge.

STRIPE PATTERN

Working in garter st, *10 rows A, 10 rows B; rep from * (20 rows) for stripe pat.

Note Instead of joining a new strand of yarn for each color change, twist A and B at the beg of every RS row to avoid long strands at edge of work.

SCARF

First corner

*With A cast on 1 st. K 1 row.

Next row K into front and back of st (inc 1)—2 sts.

Next row K1, inc 1—3 sts.

Next row K to last st, inc 1. Rep last row, working in garter st and stripe pat, until there are a total of 80 sts, end with 10 rows B.* Cut yarn. Place sts on a holder.

Second corner

Rep between *'s of first corner.

Joining row

With A, k78, SKP, pm, work sts from holder as foll: k2tog, k to last st, inc 1—159 sts. Cont in stripe pat as foll:

Next row K to last st, inc 1—160 sts.

Next row (RS) K78, SKP, sl marker, k2tog, k77, inc 1.

Next row K to last st, inc 1. Rep last 2 rows until side edge measures 80"/203cm, end with a WS row.

Center dec

Next row (RS) SKP, k to 2 sts before marker, SKP, sl marker, k2tog, k to end. Rep last row until 2 sts rem. K2tog and fasten off last st.

FINISHING

Lightly steam scarf if necessary. Do not press.

FRINGE

Cut 12"/30.5cm strands of A and B. Using 2 strands of each color, attach fringe to end of scarf. Trim ends.

Ever-decreasing ribs create interesting mitered ends on this Asian-influenced scarf, cornered with exquisite rose quartz decorative beads. A Vintage Vogue design.

KNITTED MEASUREMENTS

■ Approx 10" x 36"/25.5cm x 91.5cm

MATERIALS

■ 3 1¾oz/50g hanks (each approx 176yd/158m) of Koigu Wool Designs *Premium Merino* (wool②) in #2231 pink
■ One pair size 4 (3.5mm) needles *or size to obtain gauge*
■ Four decorative rose quartz beads

GAUGE

28 sts and 36 rows to 4"/10cm over k2, p2 rib (slightly stretched and blocked) using size 4 (3.5mm) needles.
Take time to check gauge.

HORIZONTAL RIB
Row 1 (RS) Knit.
Row 2 Purl.
Row 3 Knit.
Row 4 Knit.
Row 5 Purl.
Row 6 Knit.
Rep rows 1-6 for horizontal rib.

SCARF
Cast on 70 sts. Work 6 rows horizontal rib.
Rows 7 and 9 P2, cont horizontal rib to last 2 sts, p2.
Row 8 K2, cont horizontal rib to last 2 sts, k2.
Rows 10 and 12 K2, p2, cont horizontal rib to last 4 sts, p2, k2.
Row 11 P2, k2, cont horizontal rib to last 4 sts, k2, p2.
Rows 13 and 15 P2, k2, p2, cont horizontal rib to last 6 sts, p2, k2, p2.
Row 14 K2, p2, k2, cont horizontal rib to last 6 sts, k2, p2, k2.
Cont in pat as established, working 2 sts more in k2, p2 rib every 3rd row until all sts are in rib. Work in k2, p2 rib until piece measures 31½"/80cm from beg, end with a RS row.
Next row (WS) Work 32 sts in k2, p2 rib, p6, rib to end.
Next 2 rows K the knit sts and p the purl sts.
Row 4 Rib 30 sts, k10, rib to end.
Next 2 rows K the knit sts and p the purl sts.
Cont as established, working 4 sts more in horizontal rib at center every 3rd row until all sts are in horizontal rib and end of scarf corresponds with beg.
Bind off.

FINISHING
Block scarf. Attach a bead to each corner.

SIDEWAYS SCARF
Beyond the fringe

Stripes of rich color; soft, textural yarns and interesting stitches run lengthwise across Peggy McKenzie's artistic scarf. Hand-dyed yarns form a lush fringe.

KNITTED MEASUREMENTS

■ Approx 12" x 56"/30.5cm x 142cm (without fringe)

MATERIALS

■ 1 3½oz/100g skein (each approx 98yd/88m) of Colinette/Unique Kolours *Isis* (viscose④) each in #103 Cezanne (A) and #117 velvet bilberry (B)

■ 1 3½oz/100g skein (each approx 125yd/113m) of *Prism* (cotton⑤) in #105 Van Gogh (C)

■ 1 3½oz/100g skein (each approx 101yd/94m) of *Zanziba* (wool/viscose/nylon④) each in #102 pierro (D) and #114 velvet olive (E)

■ One pair size 10½ (6.5mm) needles *or size to obtain gauge*

■ Tapestry needle

GAUGE

9 sts and 19 rows to 4"/10cm over seed st using size 10½ (6.5mm) needles.
Take time to check gauge.

STITCH GLOSSARY

Seed Stitch

Row 1 (RS) *K1, p1; rep from * to end.
Row 2 K the purl sts and p the knit sts.
Rep row 2 for seed st.

Notes 1) Scarf is knit sideways. Cast on row is length of scarf. **2)** When changing yarns, leave 9"/23cm ends which will be incorporated into the fringe later.

SCARF

With A, loosely cast on 125 sts. Work as foll:

Rows 1-6 Work in seed st.
Row 7 (RS) With E, work 6 sts seed st, *yo, p2tog, work 5 sts seed st; rep from * to end.
Row 8 Work 5 sts seed st, *yo, p2tog, work 5 sts seed st; rep from * to last 6 sts, work 6 sts seed st.
Row 9 Rep row 7.
Row 10 Rep row 8.
Rows 11 and 12 Work in seed st with A.
Rows 13 and 14 Work in seed st with B.
Rows 15-20 Work in St st with B. Cut 6 strands D, 76"/193cm long. (One strand will be used for each row.) With tapestry needle, loosely "weave" the cut strands of D back and forth between the sts. Stagger the placement of D on each row to achieve the look of weaving.
Row 21 Work in seed st with B.
Rows 22-26 With C, p1, *yo, p2tog; rep from * to end.
Rows 27 and 28 With D knit.
Rows 29 and 30 With A knit.
Rows 31 and 32 With D knit.
Rows 33 and 34 With A knit.
Rows 35 and 36 With E knit.
Rows 37 and 38 With A knit.
Rows 39 and 40 Work in seed st with B.
Rows 41-44 Work in seed st with C.
Rows 45-47 Work in seed st with B.
Row 48 With D, knit each st by winding yarn around both needles once, then around RH needle in normal way (tighten yarn after each st).
Rows 49-51 With D purl.
Row 52 With B purl.

Rows 53-55 Cut 3 strands E, 76"/193cm long. Work as for row 15 using B for St st and E for weaving.
Row 56 With B purl.
Row 57 Work in seed st with B. Bind off loosely in seed st.

FINISHING
Fringe
Cut strands of each yarn 20"/50.5cm long for fringe. Attach fringe to each end of scarf, matching yarns and colors, incorporating loose strands already attached to scarf. Trim ends.

LACE AND LEAVES WRAP

Autumn splendor

Interlocking leaves lying on a bed of lace create a clever pattern for this versatile wrap. Knotted fringe finishes the ends. Designed by Gitta Schrade.

KNITTED MEASUREMENTS

■ Approx 22½" x 50"/61cm x 127cm (without fringe)

MATERIALS

■ 10 1¾oz/50g balls (each approx 112yd/104m) of Naturally/S.R. Kerzer *Luxury Double Knitting* (mohair⑤) in #947 terracotta

■ One pair size 4 (3.5mm) needles *or size to obtain gauge*

■ Size E/4 (3.5mm) crochet hook

GAUGE

25 sts and 30 rows = 4"/10cm over leaf chart using size 4 (3.5mm) needles.
Take time to check gauge.

SHAWL

Cast on 143 sts. P 6 rows.

Beg chart

Row 1 (RS) P3, work 1st st of chart; work

34-st rep 4 times; p3.

Row 2 and all WS rows Purl, work k1, p1 into double yo's.

Cont in chart as established, until 28 rows have been worked 13 times. P 6 rows. Bind off.

FINISHING

Block piece to measurements.

Knotted fringe

Make 4 corner fringes as foll: Cut 5 strands 19¾"/50cm long for each fringe. Fold in half and attach to corners of shawl by pulling the center of folded strands through 2nd row from cast-on/bind-off row of shawl, using crochet hook, slip ends through loop and tighten.

Make 14 fringes as foll: Cut 7 strands 19¾"/50cm long for each fringe. Attach 7 at each end of shawl (in line with tip of full leaves and in line with center of half leaves).

Using all strands from corner fringe and 7 strands from next fringe, make knot approx 3"/7.5cm down from shawl edge. Cont across always using half the strands from 2 fringes to make knot; ending with half fringe and full corner fringe tog. Trim ends.

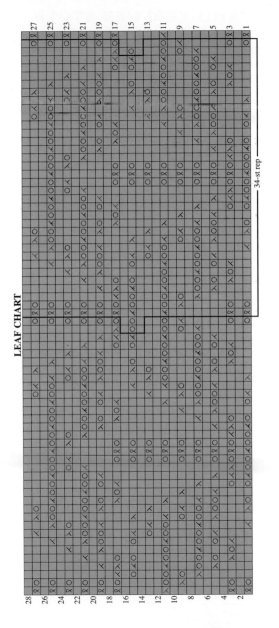

LEAF CHART

Stitch key

- ☐ K on RS, p on WS
- ☒ SK2P
- ☒ SSK
- ☒ K2tog
- ◯ Yo
- ℞ K 1tbl
- ◯◯ On WS-k into first yo; p into 2nd yo

34-st rep

Waves of blue

A basic traditional scallop pattern, also known as "fan and feather" stitch, forms an elegant evening wrap. A Vintage Vogue design.

KNITTED MEASUREMENTS

■ Approx 22" x 56"/56cm x 142cm (without fringe)

MATERIALS

■ 10 1¾oz/50g skeins (each approx 118yd/110m) of Filatura Di Crosa/Stacy Charles Collection *Fiordiloto* (viscose/silk③) in #73 blue

■ One pair size 8 (5mm) needles *or size to obtain gauge*

GAUGE

22 sts and 23 rows to 4"/10cm over scallop pat using size 8 (5mm) needles. *Take time to check gauge.*

SCALLOP PATTERN

(multiple of 17 sts)

Row 1 (RS) [K2tog] 3 times, *[yo, k1] 5 times, yo, [k2tog] 6 times; rep from *, end last rep yo, [k2tog] 3 times.

Row 2 K3, *p11, k6; rep from *, end last rep k3.

Rows 3-5 Knit.

Row 6 Purl.

Rep rows 1-6 for scallop pat.

SCARF

Cast on 119 sts and work in scallop pat for 56"/142cm, end with a pat row 6.

Bind off.

FINISHING

Block piece.

Fringe

Cut 10"/25.5cm strands. Using 2 strands for each fringe, attach fringe to each end of scarf. Trim ends.

ROSE LACE STOLE

A modern-day heirloom

Knit in whisper-fine mohair, Shirley Paden's lace stole with open and airy stitches is fine enough to slide through a wedding band.

KNITTED MEASUREMENTS
■ Approx 16" x 65"/40.5cm x 165cm

MATERIALS
■ 4 .88/25g balls (each approx 251yd/230m) of Filanda from Trendsetter Yarns *Kid Extra Fine Mohair* (mohair/nylon①) in #29 grey
■ One pair size 6 (4mm) needles *or size to obtain gauge*
■ Size E/4 (3.5mm) crochet hook
■ Small amount of a slippery waste yarn (for cast-on)
■ Stitch holder

GAUGE
21 sts and 29 rows over chart pat using size 6 (4mm) needles.
Take time to check gauge.

VANDYKE BORDER
Preparation row (WS) Knit.
Row 1 Wyib sl 1, k2, yo, k2tog, yo twice, k2tog.
Row 2 Yo, k2, p1, k2, yo, k2tog, k1.
Row 3 Wyib sl 1, k2, yo, k2tog, k4.
Row 4 K6, yo, k2tog, k1.
Row 5 Wyib sl 1, k2, yo, k2tog, [yo twice, k2tog] twice.
Row 6 K2, p1, k2, p1, k2, yo, k2tog, k1.
Row 7 Wyib sl 1, k2, yo, k2tog, k6.
Row 8 K8, yo, k2tog, k1.
Row 9 Wyib sl 1, k2, yo, k2tog, [yo twice, k2tog] 3 times.
Row 10 [K2, p1] 3 times, k2, yo, k2tog, k1.

Row 11 Wyib sl 1, k2, yo, k2tog, k9.
Row 12 Bind off 7 sts, k3, yo, k2tog, k1.

SCARF
With crochet hook and waste yarn, ch 86. With one 6 (4mm) needle, pick up and k 1 st in back lp of each ch until there are 84 sts on needle (2 extra chains rem).
Note Chain will be removed after scarf is knit.
P next row on WS.
Beg lace chart
Row 1 (RS) K1 (selvage st), work sts 1-21 of chart once, then work 20-st rep twice, then work sts 42-62 once, k1 (selvage st).
Cont in pat as established, working first and last st in garter st for selvages, until 44 rows of lace chart have been worked 9 times.
Place sts on holder.

BORDER
(make 2)
With size 6 (4mm) needles, cast on 7 sts. Work 12 rows of vandyke border 8 times. Bind off all sts.

FINISHING
Place sts from holder back on needles. With RS facing attach border to shawl as foll: Using a tapestry needle threaded with a length of mohair, place shawl on a flat surface with needle holding sts in front of border. Working loosely, beg at the right edge, sl one st from the needle onto the tapestry needle and pull the yarn through it. Pass the tapestry needle and yarn up through the first st of the bottom piece (border). Return to the top piece and sl the next st onto the tapestry needle as before, then on the border pass the tapestry needle and yarn up through the space between the first and second st.

Cont attaching the border to the shawl using the alternating grafting method as foll:

On top sl each st from needle, *on bottom*, after the first 2 attachments above, pass the tapestry needle and yarn up through one st twice, then through the space between sts, once.

Rep on the bottom 10 times as foll: *Go under one st, then the space between sts twice, then go under one st twice, then the space between.*

On the last 4 sts before the edge st go under the st, then the space between the sts on each, then go under the left edge st—36 sts picked up in the spaces between sts.

36 + 48 = 84 sts picked up in border to match 84 sts on needles.

Stitch key

☐ K on RS, p on WS

☑ Yo

◩ K2tog

◪ SKP

◪ SK2P

◪ K3tog

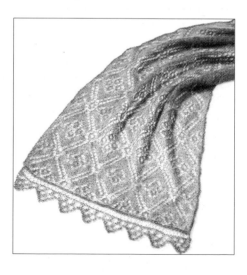

LACE CHART

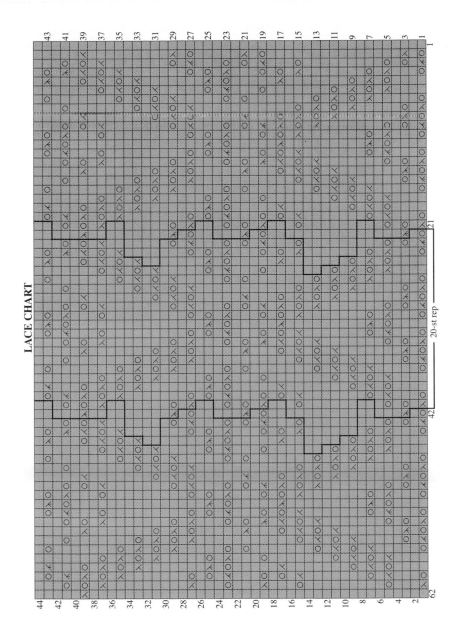

20-st rep

MOSAIC STOLE
Wrapped in luxury

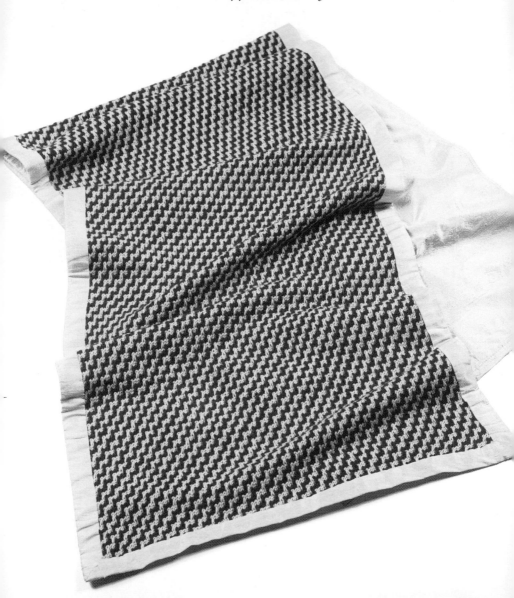

Very Easy Very Vogue

Wrap up in style with this elegant doupioni silk-lined beauty. Quick-knit glamour for all skill levels; a Vintage Vogue design.

KNITTED MEASUREMENTS
- Approx 21" x 70"/53.5cm x 177.5cm (blocked)

MATERIALS
- 5 1¾oz/50g balls (each approx 143yd/130m) of Schoeller Esslinger/Skacel *Merino Soft* (wool③) in #6 beige (A) and #12 red (B)
- One pair size 6 (4mm) needles *or size to obtain gauge*
- Size F/5 (4mm) crochet hook

GAUGE
24 sts and 32 rows to 4"/10cm over pat st using size 6 (4mm) needles.
Take time to check gauge.

PATTERN STITCH
(multiple of 4 sts plus 3)
Row 1 (RS) With B, *k3, sl 1 wyib; rep from *, end k3.
Row 2 With B, *p3, sl 1 wyif; rep from *, end p3.
Row 3 With A, sl 1 wyib, k3; rep from *, end k2.

Row 4 With A, p2, *sl 1 wyif, p3; rep from *, end sl 1.
Row 5 With B, k1, *sl 1 wyib, k3; rep from *, end k1.
Row 6 With B, p1, *sl 1 wyif, p3; rep from *, end p1.
Row 7 With A, k2, *sl 1 wyib, k3; rep from *, end sl 1.
Row 8 With A, *sl 1 wyif, p3; rep from *, end p2.
Rep rows 1-8 for pat st.

STOLE
With A, cast on 127 sts. P 1 row on WS. Work in pat st until piece measures 70"/177.5cm. Bind off with A.

FINISHING
Block stole. With RS facing, crochet hook and A, work 1 row of sc around all edges, working 3 sc in each corner.

Lining
Using stole as a pattern, cut lining from fabric plus 2"/5cm on all sides. With WS tog, baste stole and lining tog, allowing a 2"/5cm border on all edges. Turn under a ⅝"/1.5cm hem on fabric to WS and whipst to RS of stole, mitering the corners.

DIAGONAL BLOCK SCARF

It's hip to be square

Faux entrelac is surprisingly simple to knit in alternating blocks of garter and Stockinette. Soft alpaca lends drape, softness, and extra warmth. Designed by Norah Gaughan.

KNITTED MEASUREMENTS

■ Approx 10" x 45"/25.5cm x 114.5cm

MATERIALS

■ 3 1¾/50g balls (each approx 110yd/ 100m) JCA/Reynolds *Andean Alpaca* (alpaca④) in #357 seafoam

■ One pair size 7 (4.5mm) needles *or size to obtain gauge*

GAUGE

20 sts and 26 rows to 4"/10cm over St st using size 7 (4.5mm) needles.
Take time to check gauge.

SCARF

Cast on 12 sts. K 20 rows (10 ridges).
Next row Cast on 12 sts, k to end.
Next row Cast on 12 sts, k12, p12, k12— 36 sts.
Row I (RS) Knit.

Row 2 K12, p12, k12.
Rep rows 1 and 2 eight times more (10 garter ridges on RS).

Inc section
Cast on 12 sts at beg of next row and k this row.
Cast on 12 sts at beg of next row, [k12, p12] twice, k12—60 sts.
Row I Knit.
Row 2 [K12, p12] twice, k12.
Rep rows 1 and 2 eight times more.

Straight section
*When 10 garter ridges are made, cast on 12 sts at the beg of next row and k this row.
Bind off 12 sts at beg of next row, [k12, p12] twice, k12.
Work rows 1 and 2 of inc section 9 times.
Rep from * 8 times more.

Dec section
Bind off 12 sts at beg of next row and k this row.
Bind off 12 sts at the beg of next row, k12, p12, k12—36 sts.
Work rows 1 and 2 of inc section 9 times.
Bind off 12 sts at the beg of next row and knit it.
Bind off 12 sts at beg of next row, k12.
Cont to k every row until 10 garter ridges made on RS.
Bind off knitwise.

GOSSAMER SHAWL

Diamonds are a girl's best friend

Blue and white diamonds are worked in a cloud of whisper-soft mohair and silk, perfect for warming up in the evening chill. Designed by Barbara Venishnick.

KNITTED MEASUREMENTS
■ Approx 23" x 80"/58.5cm x 203cm

MATERIALS
■ 5 .88oz/25g balls (each approx 225yd/205m) of Knit One Crochet Too *Douceur et Soie* (mohair/ silk③) in #8644 blue (MC)
■ 4 balls in #8100 white (CC)
■ One pair size 3 (3mm) needles *or size to obtain gauge*
■ Size 3 (3mm) circular needle, 29"/74cm long
■ 27 small gold knitters pins

GAUGE
Each blocked diamond measures 5¾" x 5¾"/14.5cm x 14.5cm using size 3 (3mm) needles.
Take time to check gauge.

Note Each diamond is worked individually, only the final top row is worked all across.

STITCH GLOSSARY
Double decrease (double dec)
Sl 2 sts from LH to RH needle as if to k2tog, knit the next st, pass 2 sl sts over— 2 sts dec'd.

Diamond
Row I (RS) K 22 MC, k1 CC, k22 MC.
Row 2 K22 MC, p1 CC, k22 MC.
Row 3 K21 MC, double dec with CC, k21 MC.
Row 4 K21 MC, p1 CC, k21 MC.
Row 5 K20 MC, double dec with CC, k20 MC.

Row 6 K20 MC, p1 CC, k20 MC.
Row 7 K19 MC, double dec with CC, k19 MC.
Row 8 K19 MC, p1 CC, k19 MC.
Row 9 K18 MC, double dec with CC, k18 MC.
Row 10 K18 MC, p1 CC, k18 MC.
Row 11 K17 MC, double dec with CC, k17 MC.
Row 12 K17 MC, p1 CC, k17 MC.
Row 13 K16 MC, double dec with CC, k16 MC.
Row 14 K16 MC, p1 CC, k16 MC.
Row 15 K15 MC, double dec with CC, k15 MC.
Row 16 K15 MC, p1 CC, k15 MC.
Cont with CC only.
Row 17 K14, double dec, k14.
Row 18 and all WS rows Purl.
Row 19 K13, double dec, k13.
Row 21 K12, double dec, k12.
Row 23 K11, double dec, k11.
Row 25 K10, double dec, k10.
Row 27 K9, double dec, k9.
Row 29 K8, double dec, k8.
Row 31 K7, double dec, k7.
Row 33 K6, double dec, k6.
Row 35 K5, double dec, k5.
Row 37 K4, double dec, k4.
Row 39 K3, double dec, k3.
Row 41 K2, double dec, k2.
Row 43 K1, double dec, k1.
Row 45 Double dec, place last st on knitters pin, cut yarn.

SHAWL
Row I Make 14 diamonds as foll: cast on 22 sts MC, 1 CC, 22 sts MC.
Work 45 rows diamond pattern.
Row 2 First diamond With MC, pick up 22 sts along left side of one diamond, cast

on 1 st CC, with MC, pick up 22 sts along right side of another diamond. Cont the pick up as row 1 of diamond pat. Cont through row 45.

Second diamond

With MC, pick up 22 sts along left side of *row 1 diamond* just used, cast on 1 st CC, with MC, pick up 22 sts along the right side of another *row 1 diamond*, cont as for first *row 2 diamond*. Rep as for 2nd diamond until all 14 *row 1 diamonds* are attached—there are 13 *row 2 diamonds*.

Row 3 First diamond With MC, cast on 22 sts, with CC k1 from pin in top st of first *row 1 diamond*, with MC, pick up 22 sts along right side of first *row 2 diamond*, count this as row 1 of pat, cont through row 45 of diamond pat.

Second diamond

With MC, pick up 22 sts along left side of first *row 2 diamond*, with CC k1 from pin in top of next *row 1 diamond*, with MC pick up 22 sts along right side of second *row 2 diamond*—count this as row 1 of pat. Cont through row 45 as before. Cont across as for second diamond until 13 *row 3 diamonds* are complete.

Fourteenth diamond

With MC, cast on 22 sts, cut yarn. With another needle and MC, pick up 22 sts along left side of last *row 2 diamond*, with CC, k1 from pin in top of last *row 1 diamond*, with MC, k22 cast on sts. Count this as row 1 of pat. Complete diamond as before.

Rows 4 and 6 Work as for row 2.
Rows 5 and 7 Work as for row 3.

Top finishing row

Cut 27 strands of CC each approx 14"/35.5cm long. With RS facing, circular needle and MC, pick up 22 sts along RS of first diamond of row 7, k1 CC from pin at top of this diamond, with MC pick up 22 sts along left side of this first diamond, k1 CC from pin in top of first *row 6 diamond*. Rep this sequence across, never cutting color MC and using the short strands of CC for the k1 sts. End by picking up 22 sts with MC on left side of last *row 7 diamond*. Turn.

Row 1 (WS) *K22 MC, p1 CC; rep from *, end k22 MC.

Row 2 K1 MC, k2tog MC, k19 MC, *inc 1 MC, k1 CC, inc 1 MC, k21 MC, double dec CC, k21 MC; rep from *, end inc 1 MC, k1 CC, inc 1 MC, k19 MC, k2tog MC, k1 MC.

Rep these 2 rows 7 times more. With WS facing, bind off all sts knitwise.

Right side

With MC, pickup 22 sts along RS of first *row 1 diamond*, turn.

Row 1 (WS) Knit.
Row 2 K1, k2tog, k18, inc 1, k1.
Rep these 2 rows 7 times more.
With WS facing, bind off knitwise.
Sew inc edge to bottom of last *row 3 diamond*.
Rep this sequence for first row 3 and *row 5 diamonds*.

Left side

With MC, pick up 22 sts along left side of last *row 1 diamond*, turn.

Row 1 (WS) Knit.
Row 2 Inc 1, k18, k2tog, k1.
Rep these 2 rows 7 times more. With WS facing, bind off knitwise. Sew inc edge to bottom of last *row 3 diamond.*

Rep this sequence for last *row 3 and row 5 diamonds.*

FINISHING

Block piece, stretching slightly to pull out any puckering in center of diamonds.

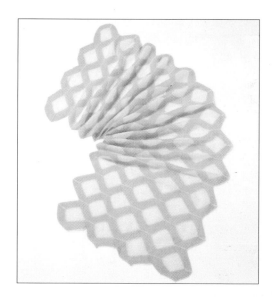

RIBBON AND EYELET SCARF
Fringe benefits

Very Easy Very Vogue

A combination of rich hand-dyed silk ribbon and a shimmery mohair blend takes basic drop stitches from simple to sublime. Designed by Fayla Reiss.

KNITTED MEASUREMENTS
■ Approx 14½" x 56"/37cm x 142cm (without fringe)

MATERIALS
■ 2 1¾oz/50g balls (each approx 90yd/81m) of Trendsetter Yarns *Dune* (mohair/acrylic/viscose/nylon/metal⑤) in #54 (A)
■ 1 ¾oz/20g ball (each approx 74yd/67m) of *Eyelash* (polyester) each in #38 (B) and #1030 (C)
■ 2 40yd/36m spools of Artemis *Hanna Silk Ribbon* (silk⑤) in rusty bucket (D)
■ 1 spool in Stonehenge (E)
■ One pair size 17 (12.75mm) needles *or size to obtain gauge*

GAUGE
6 sts to 4"/10cm and 8 rows to 5"/12.5cm over garter st pat using size 17 (12.75mm) needles.
Take time to check gauge.

Note Artemis silk ribbon is cut in approx 2yd/2m lengths. Cut ends diagonally to prevent fraying. As you are knitting, tie the ends of ribbon tog securely, using colors D and E at random. You may also tie several strands tog at one time and wind into a ball before knitting.

Garter stitch pattern
Row 1 (RS) With silk ribbon (see note), *k1, wrapping yarn 3 times around needle; rep from * to end.
Row 2 With silk ribbon, knit dropping extra wrapped sts.
Rows 3 and 4 With 1 strand each A and B held tog, knit.
Rows 5-8 Rep rows 1-4.
Rows 9 and 10 Rep rows 1 and 2.
Rows 11 and 12 With 1 strand each A and C held tog, knit.
Rows 13-16 Rep rows 9-12.
Rep rows 1-16 for garter st pat.

SCARF
With 1 strand each A and B held tog, cast on 22 sts and k 3 rows. Work in garter st pat for 68 rows. With 1 strand each A and B held tog, k 1 row. Bind off.

FINISHING
With rem yarns, cut strands 32"/81.5cm long. Use 2 strands A, 1 strand each B and C and 1 strand silk ribbon for each fringe. Attach evenly to each end of scarf (approx 13 fringe on each end). Trim to make even.

HOODED SCARF
Take cover

For Experienced Knitters

A new spin on an old favorite. Diamond-and-lace motif scarf with shaped hood and tapered ends is edged in a tiny rope cable. Designed by Joan McGowan.

KNITTED MEASUREMENTS
- Approx 12"/30.5cm wide, 34"/86.5cm long (measured from center to point)

MATERIALS
- 8 .88oz/25g balls (each approx 152yd/138m) of GGH/Muench *Soft Kid* (mohair/polyamide/wool⑤) in #13 lilac
- One pair size 10 (6mm) needles *or size to obtain gauge*
- Cable needle
- Stitch markers

GAUGE
16 sts and 24 rows to 4"/10cm over St st using size 10 (6mm) needles and 2 strands of yarn held tog.
Take time to check gauge.

Note Work with two strands of yarn held tog throughout.

STITCH GLOSSARY
3-st RPT
Sl 1 st to cn, hold to *back*, k2, p1 from cn.
3-st LPT
Sl 2 sts to cn, hold to *front*, p1, k2 from cn.
5-st LPT
Sl 3 sts to cn and hold to *front*, k2, sl p st from cn and p1, sl 2 sts from cn, k2 from cn.

6-st RC
Sl 3 sts to cn, hold to *back*, k3, k3 from cn.
6-st LC
Sl 3 sts to cn, hold to *front*, k3, k3 from cn.

SCARF
With 2 strands, cast on 19 sts.
Row I (RS) Work 3 edge sts in garter st, work 6 sts cable chart 1, p1, work 6 sts cable chart 2, work 3 edge sts in garter st. Cont in this way for 3 rows more.
Next row (RS) Work 9 sts, pm, M1 p-st, p1, M1 p-st, pm, work 9 sts. Work 3 rows even.
Next row Work 9 sts, sl marker, M1 p-st, p3, M1 p-st, sl marker, work 9 sts.
Cont in this way to inc 2 p-sts inside of markers every 7th row 6 times more, then every other row 13 times—61 sts, AT SAME TIME, when scarf measures 7"/17.5cm from beg, beg cable lace chart over center 19 sts. Cont in pat as established, until 4½ repeats of cable lace chart have been completed.
Back neck dart
Next row (RS) Bind off 9 sts, work to end. Cont to dec 1 st at beg of every RS row, until 30 rows of 5th cable lace motif have been worked. Inc 1 st in last st at end of every WS row 7 times, then cast on 9 sts for cable and edge sts.
Work other side to correspond, reversing dart shaping.
Bind off in pat.
FINISHING
Turn edge sts to WS and sew in place. Sew center back dart. Sew tog cable at ends to form points. Block scarf.

CABLE LACE CHART

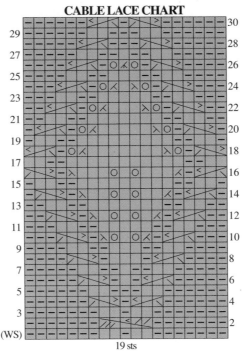

19 sts

Color key

▦	K on RS, p on WS
—	P on RS, k on WS
O	Yo
◿	K2tog
◼	SKP
◪	Double dec
◢◣	3-st RPT
◣◢	3-st LPT
◢◣	5-st LPT
◢◢◣	6-st RC
◢◣◣	6-st LC

CABLE CHART 1

6 sts

CABLE CHART 2

6 sts

LEAF AND CABLE SCARF
Fall foliage

For Intermediate Knitters

Panels of cascading leaves bordered by rope cables are trimmed with striped fringe. This fitting tribute to autumn was designed by Sasha Kagan.

KNITTED MEASUREMENTS

 Approx 10¾" x 59"/27.5cm x 150cm (without fringe)

MATERIALS

 7 .88oz/25g balls (each approx 75yd/67m) of Rowan/Westminster Fibers *Lightweight DK* (wool③) in #140 dk olive (A)

 1 1¾oz/50g balls (each approx 190yd/175m) of *DK Soft* (wool/polyamide③) in #175 sage (B)

 2 .88oz/25g balls (each approx 70yd/63m) of *Kid Silk* (mohair/silk③) each in #989 gold (C) and #972 lt brown (D)

 1 1¾oz/50g balls (each approx 173yd/160m) of *Fine Cotton Chenille* (cotton/polyester③) each in #409 plum (E), #408 crocus (F) and #411 pale green (G)

 One pair size 5 (3.75mm) needles *or size to obtain gauge*

 Cable needle

GAUGE

32 sts and 30 rows to 4"/10cm over chart pat using size 5 (3.75mm) needles.
Take time to check gauge.

STITCH GLOSSARY

4-st RC

Sl 2 sts to cn and hold to *back*, k2, k2 from cn.

4-st LC

Sl 2 sts to cn and hold to *front*, k2, k2 from cn.

Notes 1) When changing colors, twist yarns on WS to prevent holes in work. **2)** Sl the first st of every row to make a firm edge at both sides of scarf.

SCARF

With A, cast on 86 sts. Work in leaf and cable chart until piece measures 59"/150cm from beg, end with a RS row. Bind off.

FINISHING

Block scarf.

Fringe

Cut 8"/20.5cm strands of A, C and D. Using 10 strands for each fringe, attach 17 fringe to each end of scarf in foll color sequence: [A, C, A, D] 4 times, A. Trim ends.

74

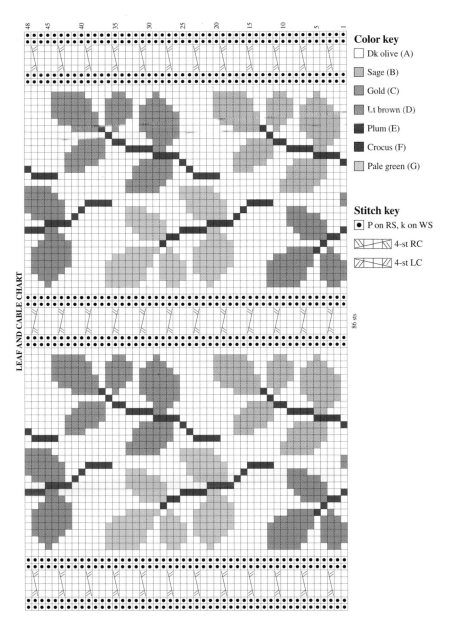

Color key

- ☐ Dk olive (A)
- ▨ Sage (B)
- ▨ Gold (C)
- ▨ Lt brown (D)
- ■ Plum (E)
- ■ Crocus (F)
- ▨ Pale green (G)

Stitch key

- ⊙ P on RS, k on WS
- ⧄⧄ 4-st RC
- ⧅⧅ 4-st LC

LEAF AND CABLE CHART

86 sts

Rib knit scarf with patterned borders is rendered in muted earth tones. A direct descendant of an antique Turkish rug, the pattern's geometric symmetry speaks the language of a rich tradition. Designed by Mari Lynn Patrick.

KNITTED MEASUREMENTS

■ Approx 10" x 65"/25cm x 165cm (without fringe)

MATERIALS

■ 3 3½oz/100g hanks (each approx 220yd/200m) of Cascade *Cascade 220* (wool④) in #9403 tan marl (MC)

■ 1 hank each in #7822 dk brown (A), #8010 ecru (B), #8555 black (C), #8686 med brown (D) and #7821 tan (E)

■ One pair each sizes 6 and 8 (4 and 5mm) needles *or size to obtain gauge*

GAUGES

■ 20 sts and 22 rows to 4"/10cm over St st and pat foll chart using larger needles.

■ 24 sts and 28 rows to 4"/10cm over k1, p1 rib using larger needles.

Take time to check gauges.

SCARF

Beg at one end with larger needles and A, cast on 50 sts.

Row 1 (RS) *With A, p2, with MC, k1; rep from *, end with A, p2.

Row 2 *With A, k2, with MC, p1; rep from *, end with A, k2.

Beg chart pat

Row 1 (RS) P1 (selvage st), beg with st 2, work in St st and row 1 of chart to last st, p1 (selvage st). Cont with selvage sts (in colors on chart) and foll chart through row 38.

+Next row (RS) *With A, k2, with MC, k1, rep from *, end with A, k2.

Next row (WS) *With A, k2, with MC, p1; rep from *, end with A, k2.

Next row (RS) *With A, p2, with MC, k1; rep from *, end with A, p2+.

Next row (WS) With A, purl.

Next row (RS) With MC, cast on 2 sts at beg of row, k to end inc 7 sts evenly spaced, and inc 2 sts in last st—61 sts.

Next row (WS) *K1, p1; rep from * end k1.

Next row K1, *p1, k1; rep from * to end. Rep these 2 rows for k1, p1 rib until piece measures 57"/144.5cm from beg.

Next row (RS) With MC, bind off 2 sts at beg of row, k across dec 7 sts evenly spaced and k last 3 sts tog—50 sts. P1 row with A. Rep between +'s once. Then foll chart in reverse (from rows 38 through 1). Rep between +'s once. Bind off with A.

FINISHING

Block flat to measurements. With smaller needles and MC, pick up and k 36 sts evenly in selvage sts along one side edge of border. Bind off knitwise on WS. Work other side edges of border in same way. Sew neatly to beg of ribbed pattern.

FRINGE

Cut 12 lengths of MC, 15"/38cm long for each fringe and pull 9 fringes through alternating color A blocks on each lower edge (knot should form on WS as in photo).

Color key

- ☐ Tan marl (MC)
- ■ Black (C)
- ■ Dk brown (A)
- ■ Med brown (D)
- ☐ Ecru (B)
- ■ Tan (E)

CHART PATTERN

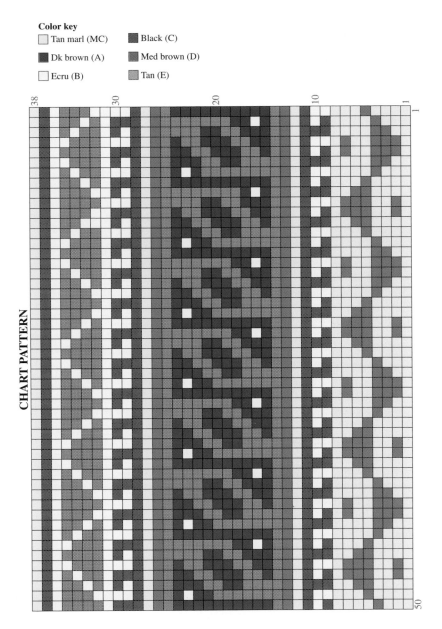

CHILD'S SHEEP SCARF

I love ewe!

Whimsical wooly sheep graze along the ends of heathery wool scarf with seed-stitch borders. Designed by Amy Bahrt.

KNITTED MEASUREMENTS
■ Approx 7" x 52"/17.5cm x 132cm

MATERIALS
■ 2 4oz/113g skeins (each approx 190yd/173m) of Brown Sheep *Lamb's Pride Worsted* (wool/mohair④) in #M-130 silver (MC)
■ 1 skein each in #M-04 charcoal heather (A), #M-180 ruby red (B) and #M-115 oatmeal (C)
■ One pair size 7 (4.5mm) needles *or size to obtain gauge*
■ Size G/6 (4.5mm) crochet hook

GAUGE
20 sts and 24 rows to 4"/10cm over St st using size 7 (4.5mm) needles.
Take time to check gauge.

SEED STITCH
Row 1 (RS) *K1, p1; rep from * to end.
Row 2 K the purl sts and p the knit sts.
Rep row 2 for seed st.

SCARF
With A cast on 35 sts. Work in seed st for ¾"/2cm, end with a WS row.
Next row (RS) Cont 3 sts in seed st, work next 29 sts in St st, cont last 3 sts in seed st.
Rep last row 3 times more.

Beg sheep chart
Row 1 (RS) Work 7 sts as established, work next 10 sts foll sheep chart, work to end. Cont in this way through chart row 12. Work 1 row with A.
Row 14 (WS) Work 6 sts as established, reading chart from left to right, work 10 sts sheep chart, work to end. Cont in this way through chart row 12. Work 4 rows A, 2 rows B. Change to MC.

Beg St st/Seed st
Row 1 (WS) Cont 3 sts in seed st, [work 5 sts in St st, 3 sts in seed st] 4 times. Cont in St st/seed st as established until piece measures 46"/117cm from beg, end with a WS row.
Cont working 3 sts each side in seed st and rem st st in St st, work 2 rows B, 4 rows A.

Beg sheep chart
Note Turn chart upside down and read chart from row 12 to row 1 to reverse direction of sheep.
Row 1 (RS) Work 6 sts as established, work 10 sts sheep chart, work to end. Cont in this way through chart row 1. Work 1 row even.
Next row (WS) Work 7 sts, with chart turned upside down and reading from left to right, work 10 sts sheep chart, work to end. Cont in this way through chart row 1. Work 4 rows A. Work all sts in seed st with A for ¾"/2cm.
Bind off all sts in pat.

FINISHING
Block piece lightly.

Lamb's ears
With crochet hook, join a strand of B at point on chart, ch 5 loosely, fold in half and join again at starting point.

SHEEP CHART

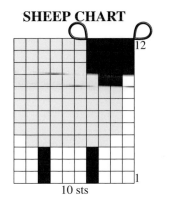

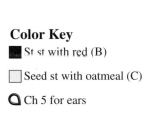

12

1

10 sts

Color Key

■ St st with red (B)

☐ Seed st with oatmeal (C)

◖ Ch 5 for ears

FAIR ISLE SCARF
Shades of the Shetlands

For Intermediate Knitters

Folded double for extra warmth, this handsome Fair Isle scarf, knit in rich earth tones, will keep out the cold on the most blustery of days. Designed by Vladimir Teriokhin.

KNITTED MEASUREMENTS

▩ Approx 7" x 48"/17.5cm x 122cm

MATERIALS

▩ 4 1¾oz/50g balls (each approx 110yd/100m) of Dale of Norway *Heilo* (wool③) in #0007 grey (MC)

▩ 2 balls each in #3152 tan (A), #0083 dk grey (B), #3481 brown (C) and #0017 ecru (D)

▩ One pair size 5 (3.75mm) needles *or size to obtain gauge*

▩ Cable needle

GAUGE

16 sts and 26 rows to 4"/10cm over chart pats using size 5 (3.75mm) needles.
Take time to check gauge.

SCARF

With MC, cast on 60 sts.

***Beg chart 1**

Row 1 (RS) With MC, work 10-st rep 6 times. Cont as established through row 20.

Beg chart 2

Row 1 (RS) Work 12-st rep 5 times. Cont as established through row 23. Change to MC.

Beg chart 3

Row 1 (WS) With MC, p2, work 7-st rep 8 times, p2. Cont in pat as established, working first and last st in St st, through chart row 20.

Beg chart 4

Row 1 (WS) Work same as chart 2.

Rep from * (86 rows) twice more, then work charts 1, 2 and 3 once more. Bind off.

FINISHING

Block scarf. With WS tog, fold in half and sew 3 sides.

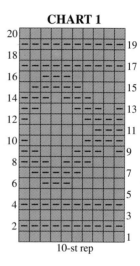

CHART 1

10-st rep

Stitch key

▩ K on RS, p on WS

⊟ P on RS, k on WS

CHART 2

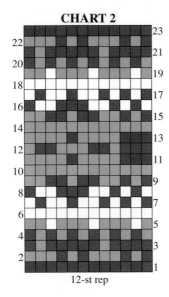

12-st rep

CHART 3

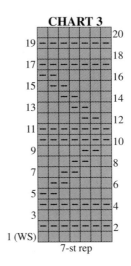

7-st rep

CHART 4

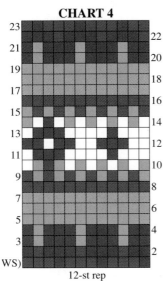

12-st rep

Stitch key

▨ K on RS, p on WS

▭ P on RS, k on WS

Color key

▨ Grey (MC)

▢ Tan (A)

▨ Dk grey (B)

▨ Brown (C)

▢ Ecru (D)

DRAGONFLY SHAWL
The secret garden

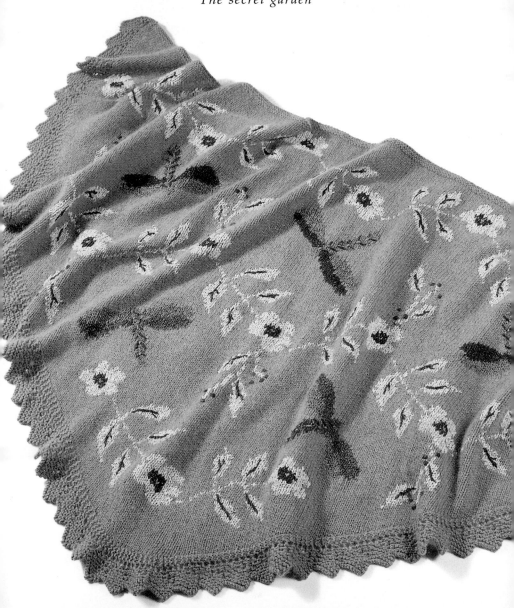

Pam Allen captures the magic of a summer evening. This shawl, scattered with intarsia or duplicate stitch dragonflies and flowering vines, is trimmed with a knitted lace border.

KNITTED MEASUREMENTS

- Approx 75" x 36"/190.5cm x 91.5cm (including border)

MATERIALS

- 8 1¾oz/50g balls (each approx 140yd/135m) of Tahki Imports *Sable* (wool/angora④) in #1640 taupe (MC)
- 2 1¾oz/50g balls (each approx 105yd/96m) of Tahki Imports *Chelsea Silk* (silk/wool④) in #166A oatmeal (A)
- 1 ball each in #120A teal (B) 121 purple (C) and #112A gold (D)
- One size 8 (5mm) circular needle *or size to obtain gauge*
- Size E/4 (3.5mm) crochet hook

GAUGE

18 sts and 24 rows = 4"/10cm over St st using size 8 (5mm) needles.
Take time to check gauge.

Notes 1) Shawl is worked back and forth on a circular needle to accommodate the large number of sts. **2)** The shaping of the shawl is shown on the placement diagram. The placement of the various charts are also shown on this diagram. The individual charts are drawn separately for easy reading. **3)** Chart 1 is knit in. Dragonfly and vines (charts 2, 3 and 4) are worked in duplicate st after piece is complete.

SHAWL

With MC, cast on 18 sts.
Row 1 (RS) Knit.
Row 2 Cast on 3 sts, p to end.
Cont in St st, casting on 3 sts at beg of next 5 rows—36 sts.
Next (inc) row (WS) Inc 1 st in first st, work to last st, inc 1 st in last st. Cont in St st, inc 1 st each side *every* row until there are 50 sts.

Beg chart 1
Row 15 (RS) Work inc, then counting inc st, beg with st 14 and work row 1 of chart 1 through st 65—52 sts. Cont in pat as established (working inc sts into chart), through row 42 of chart. Cont to inc 1 st each side *every* row until there are 92 sts, then work inc every RS row until there are 318 sts, then work 4 rows even, AT SAME TIME, work reps of chart 1 as shown on placement diagram. Bind off.

FINISHING
Block piece to measurements. Work charts 2, 3 and 4 in duplicate st and French knots, reversing and turning charts as shown in photo or as desired. (**Note:** colors of dragonfly varies. See photo for color or work as desired.) Work satin st embroidery on dragonflies and leaves as shown.

Edging
With MC, cast on 10 sts.
Row 1 (RS) P3, yo, p7.
Row 2 P7, yo, p4.
Row 3 P3, yo, k2tog, yo, p7.
Row 4 P7, yo, k2tog, yo, p4.
Row 5 P3, [yo, k2tog] twice, yo, p7.
Row 6 P7, [yo, k2tog] twice, yo, p4.
Row 7 P3, [yo, k2tog] 3 times, yo, p7.
Row 8 Bind off 7 purlwise, p to end.
Rep rows 1-8 until straight edge fits along sides on shawl. Bind off and sew in place.

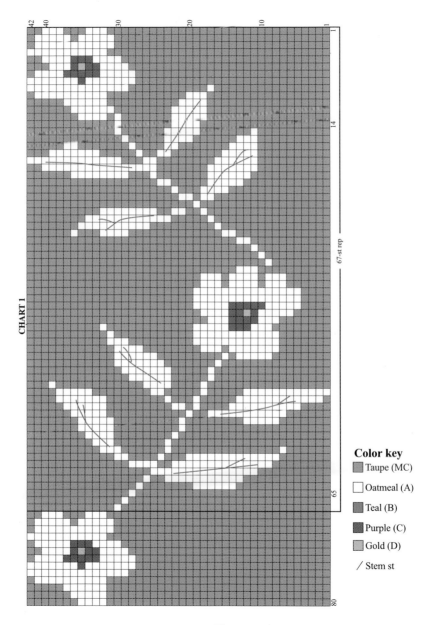

CHART 1

67-st rep

Color key

- ▨ Taupe (MC)
- ☐ Oatmeal (A)
- ▨ Teal (B)
- ▨ Purple (C)
- ▨ Gold (D)
- ╱ Stem st

PLACEMENT

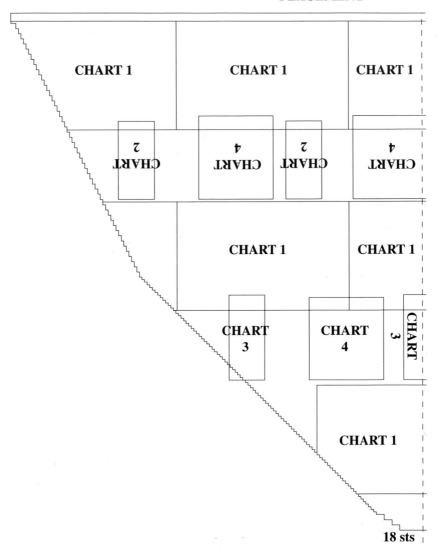

DIAGRAM

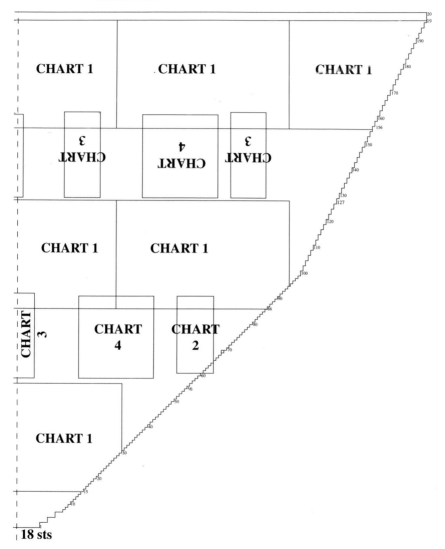

CHART 1   CHART 1   CHART 1

CHART 3   CHART 4   CHART 3

CHART 1   CHART 1

CHART 3   CHART 4   CHART 2

CHART 1

18 sts

CHART 2

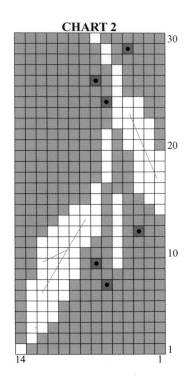

30

20

10

1

14   1

CHART 3

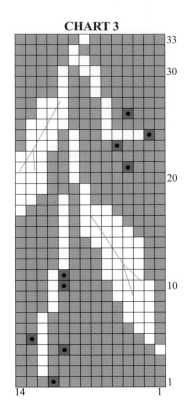

33

30

20

10

1

14   1

Color key

☐ Taupe (MC)

☐ Oatmeal (A)

■ Teal (B)

■ Purple (C)

● French knot with purple (C)

☐ Gold (D)

╱ Stem st

CHART 4

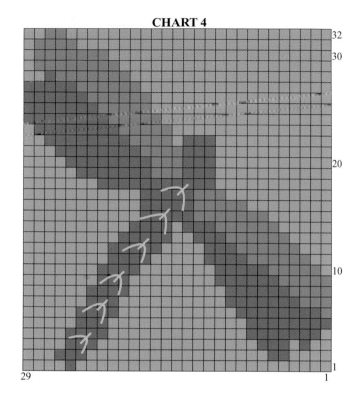

32
30

20

10

1
1

29

NOTES

NOTES

RESOURCES

US RESOURCES

Write to the yarn companies listed below for purchasing and mail-order information.

ADRIENNE VITTADINI
distributed by
JCA

ARTEMIS
179 High Street
S. Portland, MN 04106
(888) 233-5187

AURORA YARNS
PO Box 3068
Moss Beach, CA 94038

BAABAJOES WOOL COMPANY
P O Box 260604
Lakewood, CO 80226
www.baabajoeswool.com

BARUFFA
distributed by
Lane Borgosesia

BERROCO, INC.
PO Box 367
Uxbridge, MA 01569

BROWN SHEEP CO., INC.
100662 County Road 16
Mitchell, NE 69357

CASCADE YARNS, INC.
2401 Utah Ave. S
Suite 505
Seattle, WA 98134

CLASSIC ELITE YARNS
300A Jackson Street
Lowell, MA 01852
www.classiceliteyarns.com

CLECKHEATON
distributed by
Plymouth Yarn

COLINETTE YARNS
distributed by
Unique Kolours

DALE OF NORWAY, INC.
N16 W 23390 Stoneridge Dr.
Suite A
Waukesha, WI 53188

FILANDA
distributed by
Trendsetter Yarns

FILATURA DI CROSA
distributed by
Stacy Charles Collection

FINGERLAKES WOOLEN MILL
1193 Stewarts Corners Road
Genoa, NY 13071
www.fingerlakes-yarns.com

GREAT ADIRONDACK YARN COMPANY
950 County Hwy. 126
Amsterdam, NY 12010

GARNSTUDIO
distributed by
Aurora Yarns

JCA
35 Scales Lane
Townsend, MA 01469

KIC2 SOLUTIONS
2220 Eastman Ave. #105
Ventura, CA 93003

KOIGU WOOL DESIGNS
R. R. #1
Williamsford, ON N0H 2V0
Canada

LANE BORGOSESIA
PO Box 217
Colorado Springs, CO 80903

LION BRAND YARNS
34 West 15th Street
New York, NY 10011
www.lionbrand.com

MUENCH YARNS
285 Bel Marin Keys Blvd. Unit J
Novato, CA 94949

NATURALLY
distributed
S. R. Kertzer

PLYMOUTH YARN
PO Box 28
Bristol, PA 19007

ROWAN
distributed by
Westminster Fibers

S. R. KERTZER
105A Winges Road
Woodbridge, ON L4L 6C2
Canada

SCHAFFHAUSER
distributed by
Skacel Collection

SKACEL COLLECTION
PO Box 88110
Seattle, WA 98138-2110

STACY CHARLES COLLECTION
1059/1061 Manhattan Ave.
Brooklyn, NY 11222

TAHKI IMPORTS, LTD.
11 Graphic Place
Moonachie, NJ 07074
www.tahki.com

TRENDSETTER YARNS
16742 Stagg Street
Suite 104
Van Nuys, CA 91406

UNIQUE KOLOURS
1428 Oak Lane
Downingtown, PA 19335

WESTMINSTER FIBERS
5 Northern Blvd.
Amherst, NH 03031

WOOL PAK YARNS NZ
distributed by
Baabajoes Wool Company

CANADIAN RESOURCES

Write to US resources for mail-order availability of yarns not listed.

BERROCO, INC.
distributed by
R. Stein Yarn Corp.

CLASSIC ELITE YARNS
distributed by
S. R. Kertzer, Ltd.

CLECKHEATON
distributed by
Diamond Yarn

COLINETTE YARNS
distributed by
Diamond Yarn

DIAMOND YARN
9697 St. Lauren
Montreal, PQ H3L 2N1

ESTELLE DESIGNS & SALES, LTD.
Units 65/67
2220 Midland Ave.
Scarborough, ON M1P 3E6

FILATURA DI CROSA
distributed by
Diamond Yarn

KOIGU WOOL DESIGNS
R. R. #1
Williamsford, ON N0H 2V0

NATURALLY
distributed by
S. R. Kertzer

R. STEIN YARN CORP.
5800 St-Denis
Suite 303
Montreal, PQ H2S 3L5

ROWAN
distributed by
Diamond Yarn

S. R. KERTZER, LTD.
105A Winges Rd.
Woodbridge, ON L4L 6C2

UK RESOURCES

Not all yarns used in this book are available in the UK. For yarns not available, make a comparable substitute or contact the US manufacturer for purchasing and mail-order information.

COATS CRAFTS UK
distributors of Patons
PO Box 22
The Lingfield Estate
Darlington
Co Durham DL1 1YQ
Tel: 01325-365457

COLINETTE YARNS, LTD.
Units 2-5
Banwy Industrial Estate
Llanfair Caereinion
Powys SY21 OSG
Tel: 01938-810128

ROWAN YARNS
Green Lane Mill
Holmfirth
West Yorks HD7 1RW
Tel: 01484-681881

SILKSTONE
12 Market Place
Cockermouth
Cumbria, CA13 9NQ
Tel: 01900-821052

VOGUE KNITTING SCARVES

Editor-in-Chief
TRISHA MALCOLM

Art Director
CHRISTINE LIPERT

Senior Editor
CARLA S. SCOTT

Managing Editor
DARYL BROWER

Technical Illustration Editor/
Page Layout
ELIZABETH BERRY

Knitting Coordinator
JEAN GUIRGUIS

Yarn Coordinator
VERONICA MANNO

Instructions Coordinators
CHARLOTTE PARRY
KAREN GREENWALD

Editorial Coordinators
KATHLEEN KELLY
ELLEN LESPERANCE

Photography
BRIAN KRAUS, NYC
Photographed at Butterick Studios

Project Director
CAROLINE POLITI

Production Managers
LILLIAN ESPOSITO
WINNIE HINISH

Publishing Consultant
MIKE SHATZKIN, THE IDEALOGICAL COMPANY

President, Sixth&Spring Books
ART JOINNIDES